Introduction

Welcome to a world where culinary art meets science,
delight. Imagine aromatic, juicy dishes with a rich flavor where every note retains its natural essence. This is the magic of sous vide technology.

When you immerse yourself in the process of cooking with sous vide, you become the master of your own gastronomic world. You take simple yet fresh ingredients and transform them into works of art, preserving vitamins, minerals, and everything that makes food not only tasty but also healthy.

In this book, we reveal the secrets of preparing dishes that fill your home with aromas akin to the finest restaurants in the world. You will learn how to achieve perfect texture and flavor, how to preserve the natural composition of the ingredients, and make every dish a masterpiece worthy of admiration.

This book is your guide to a world of healthy and delicious food. It is created for those who strive for culinary perfection, for those who want to delight their loved ones with not only tasty but also healthy dishes. Here, you will find recipes that will become the foundation of your daily diet, bringing joy and health to each of your days.

Discover the secret to juicy dishes with rich aroma and flavor, preserving their natural essence. Let this book become your indispensable assistant on the path to a healthy and happy future.

With best wishes,

Yurii Sreda

Table of Contents

Understanding Sous Vide

1. What is Sous Vide?

1.1 History and Development of Sous Vide Technology

Sous Vide, which translates from French as "under vacuum," is a cooking method that was developed in the mid-1970s. Initially, this technique was used in high-end restaurants to achieve an unparalleled level of control over the cooking process and to ensure perfect texture and flavor in dishes.

Historical Roots:

- **1970s:** French chefs began experimenting with the use of vacuum bags and low-temperature cooking. One of the pioneers of Sous Vide was Georges Pralus, a chef at the restaurant Troisgros in Roanne, France. Pralus noticed that cooking foie gras in vacuum packaging at a low temperature preserved its texture and flavor better than traditional methods.
- **1980s:** Sous Vide gained popularity in professional kitchens worldwide, especially in France and the United States. During this period, the technology was refined and adapted for various types of products.
- **1990s:** Sous Vide began to be used in mass food production to improve consistency and extend shelf life.
- **2000s:** With the advent of affordable home Sous Vide devices, this technology became popular among home cooks and healthy eating enthusiasts.

1.2. Modern Use

Restaurants: Imagine a restaurant where every bite of food melts in your mouth, revealing a rich and intense flavor. Sous vide is the magical key to culinary perfection, used by chefs around the world, from luxurious fine-dining establishments to cozy cafes. This technique allows chefs to prepare dishes in advance, maintaining their freshness and serving them at the perfect moment. In every restaurant that uses sous vide, you can be sure of the ideal texture and aroma of each dish.

Home Kitchens: Imagine a small miracle happening in your kitchen. Modern household sous vide devices have made this advanced technology accessible to everyone. Sous vide has become an integral part of the lives of home cooks striving for professional results. Now, anyone can enjoy juicy and aromatic dishes prepared with love and attention to detail, without leaving their home.

Sous vide opens the doors to new gastronomic adventures, allowing you to cook food at precise temperatures that are impossible to achieve with traditional methods. This method provides the opportunity to experiment with new flavors and textures, turning every meal into a true culinary masterpiece. Sous vide is more than just a cooking method; it is a path to creating perfect dishes, rich in aroma and flavor, while preserving the natural essence of each ingredient.

1.3. Basic Principles

Sous Vide is a cooking method that relies on precise temperature control to achieve the best results. This method reveals the magic of each ingredient by following several key principles:

1.3.1. Temperature Control

Temperature plays a crucial role in the Sous Vide process. Unlike traditional cooking methods where temperature can vary significantly, Sous Vide allows food to be cooked at a stable, precisely controlled temperature. This is achieved using a circulator that maintains the water in the container at the set temperature for extended periods. This means you can cook a steak at 131°F (55°C) and it will be evenly cooked to a perfect medium-rare throughout. This ensures ideal texture and flavor while preserving all the nutrients.

1.3.2. Vacuum Sealing

Food is hermetically sealed in vacuum bags, preventing contact with air and retaining moisture, aromas, and nutrients within the product. Vacuum sealing also inhibits bacterial growth, making the cooking process safer. Special vacuum sealers and airtight bags are used for this purpose. This helps preserve the natural juiciness and aroma of each ingredient.

1.3.3. Prolonged Cooking

One of the main advantages of Sous Vide is the ability to cook food for extended periods at low temperatures. This method allows cooking for several hours or even days without the risk of overcooking. Prolonged cooking at low temperatures enables proteins and fat cells to break down slowly, enhancing the texture and flavor of the dish. For example, a beef steak cooked using the Sous Vide method will have a perfectly tender texture and rich flavor. This method ensures tenderness and juiciness in dishes that are difficult to achieve with traditional methods.

2. Advantages of the Method

Sous Vide reveals numerous advantages that make it indispensable in the kitchen for both professional chefs and home cooks.

Even Cooking: Sous Vide ensures even cooking throughout the thickness of the product. This is particularly important for large cuts of meat or fish, where traditional methods often result in overcooked exteriors and undercooked interiors. Sous Vide guarantees perfect texture and juiciness in every bite.

Nutrient Preservation: Cooking at low temperatures allows for the retention of more vitamins and minerals compared to traditional methods. Food is cooked in hermetically sealed bags, which minimizes nutrient loss. This makes dishes not only delicious but also nutritious.

Intensity of Flavor: Vacuum sealing preserves all the aromas within the product, creating rich and flavorful dishes. Each ingredient retains its natural essence, and spices and marinades penetrate deeper, making the flavor more vibrant and intense.

Minimization of Waste: Since food is cooked in vacuum bags, the risk of drying out or overcooking is minimized. This helps prevent food waste and saves ingredients. Every piece remains juicy and tender, even after prolonged cooking.

Extended Shelf Life of Prepared Dishes: Dishes prepared using the Sous Vide method can be stored in vacuum-sealed bags for an extended period. This allows for advance preparation and storage of dishes until they are needed. Prepared dishes can be easily reheated or finished just before serving, maintaining their freshness and flavor.

Pre-Marinating: Sous Vide allows you to prepare portions of dishes in advance by adding spices and vacuum-sealing them. This not only saves time but also enhances the flavor and aroma of the dish. Marinades penetrate deeper into the product, making the taste richer.

Time Efficiency: Sous Vide saves time by allowing dishes to be cooked overnight or in advance. If a dish requires long cooking times, you can start the process in the evening and have a ready meal by morning. This is especially convenient for busy people who want to enjoy tasty and healthy food without extra hassle.

Maximum Health Benefits: Sous Vide helps prepare dishes that retain the maximum amount of nutrients and exclude harmful processes, such as glycation. Glycation is a reaction between sugar and proteins that occurs at high temperatures and can lead to the formation of harmful substances in food. Thanks to low-temperature cooking, Sous Vide avoids glycation, making dishes healthier and safer.

These advantages make Sous Vide not just a cooking method, but a true culinary art that brings pleasure and health to every meal.

3. Equipment for Sous Vide

Cooking with the Sous Vide method requires specialized equipment that helps maintain precise temperatures and hermetically seal food. Here's what you'll need:

3.1. Essential Equipment

3.1.1. Sous Vide Machine (Circulator)

A Sous Vide machine or circulator is a device that maintains a stable water temperature throughout the cooking process. The circulator heats the water and keeps it circulating, ensuring even cooking. When choosing a Sous Vide machine, consider the following features:

- **Temperature Range and Accuracy:** Look for a circulator with a wide temperature range and high accuracy to cook various products.
- **Power:** Powerful models heat water faster and maintain a stable temperature even with large volumes of water.
- **Ease of Use:** Look for features like a digital display, timer, and remote control capabilities via a mobile app.

Here are the main types of Sous Vide equipment:

1. **Immersion Circulators** These devices attach to the edge of a pot or container filled with water. They heat and circulate the water to maintain an even temperature.
   - **Advantages:** Compact, can be used with various containers, easy to store.
   - **Disadvantages:** Requires a separate water container.
2. **Water Ovens** These devices have an integrated water container, often with a lid to prevent evaporation.
   - **Advantages:** Easy to use, convenient, precise temperature control.
   - **Disadvantages:** Takes up more storage space, limited cooking volume.
3. **Home Sous Vide Devices** These are designed for home use and can be either immersion circulators or water ovens.
   - **Advantages:** Affordable, easy to use.
   - **Disadvantages:** Limited power, less durable compared to professional models.

4. **Industrial (Professional) Sous Vide Devices** These are intended for restaurants and professional kitchens. They often have larger capacities, higher power, and additional features.
   o **Advantages:** High performance, durability, ability to cook large quantities.
   o **Disadvantages:** High cost, large size.
5. **Multifunctional Devices** Some modern multi-cookers and ovens have a Sous Vide mode, making them multifunctional.
   o **Advantages:** Space-saving, multiple functionalities.
   o **Disadvantages:** Less precise temperature control compared to specialized Sous Vide devices.

3.1.2. Vacuum Sealer

Vacuum sealers play a crucial role in the Sous Vide cooking process, as they allow you to remove air from food bags and seal them hermetically. This is necessary to prevent oxidation and ensure that the food is in close contact with water. There are different types of vacuum sealers, each with its own features and suitable for various needs. Here are the main types of vacuum sealers for Sous Vide:

1. **Chamber Vacuum Sealers** These devices have a chamber where the bag with the product is placed. The chamber creates a vacuum both inside and around the bag and then seals it.
   o **Advantages:** High level of vacuuming, ability to package liquids and marinades, reliability.
   o **Disadvantages:** High cost, large size, heavy weight.
2. **External Vacuum Sealers** These devices work by sucking air out of the bag, which remains outside the machine. They are usually more compact and cheaper.
   o **Advantages:** Compactness, affordable price, ease of use.
   o **Disadvantages:** Limited ability to handle liquids, lower vacuuming power compared to chamber sealers.

3. **Handheld Vacuum Sealers** These small devices are used to vacuum special bags with valves or containers. They are portable and convenient for small volumes of food.

- o **Advantages:** Portability, ease of use, affordable price.
- o **Disadvantages:** Limited power, less reliable vacuuming.
4. **Combination Vacuum Sealers** These devices combine the functions of vacuuming and sealing and may include both external and chamber mechanisms in one unit.
    - o **Advantages:** Versatility, ability to work with different types of bags and products.
    - o **Disadvantages:** Higher price, can be bulkier.
5. **Vacuum Canister Sealers** These devices are specifically designed for vacuuming containers and jars. They are often used for storing dry goods and liquids.

- o **Advantages:** Ability to work with rigid containers, convenience in storing products.
- o **Disadvantages:** Not suitable for all types of products, requires additional accessories.
6. **Commercial Vacuum Sealers** These devices are intended for use in professional kitchens and the food industry. They have high power and can handle large volumes of products.
    - o **Advantages:** High performance, reliability, durability.
    - o **Disadvantages:** High cost, large size.

3.1.3. Sous Vide Containers and Baths

Sous Vide containers and baths are essential accessories used with immersion circulators for Sous Vide cooking. They help maintain a stable water temperature and ensure even cooking of the food. Here are the main types of Sous Vide containers and baths, their features, and benefits:

1. Polycarbonate Containers These containers are made of durable and heat-resistant polycarbonate and are often used with immersion circulators.

- **Advantages:**
    - o Transparency allows you to monitor the cooking process.
    - o Lightweight and durable.
    - o Wide range of sizes.
- **Disadvantages:**
    - o Can be prone to scratching.
    - o Require additional insulation to reduce heat loss.

2. Stainless Steel Containers These containers are made of stainless steel, making them durable and resistant to corrosion.

- **Advantages:**
    - o High strength and durability.
    - o Excellent thermal insulation.
    - o Hygienic and easy to clean.

- **Disadvantages:**
  - Higher cost.
  - Heavier than plastic counterparts.

3. Insulated Containers These containers have additional insulation to minimize heat loss and maintain a stable water temperature.

- **Advantages:**
  - Energy savings.
  - Reduced water heating time.
  - More stable cooking temperature.
- **Disadvantages:**
  - Higher cost.
  - Limited selection of models and sizes.

4. Food Grade Thermo Containers These containers have food-grade insulation and are often used in professional kitchens.

- **Advantages:**
  - Maintain a stable temperature for extended periods.
  - Safe for food.
  - Often equipped with lids to reduce evaporation.
- **Disadvantages:**
  - Expensive.
  - Take up a lot of space.

5. Collapsible Containers These containers can be collapsed for convenient storage when not in use.

- **Advantages:**
  - Space-saving.
  - Easy to transport.
  - Convenient storage.
- **Disadvantages:**
  - May be less stable.
  - Limited selection of sizes and models.

6. Containers with Lids and Accessories Many containers come with lids that help reduce water evaporation and retain heat. Some also have special slots for immersion circulators.

- **Advantages:**
  - Reduced water evaporation.
  - Maintained stable temperature.
  - Can be used with various accessories (racks, bag holders, etc.).
- **Disadvantages:**
  - Additional accessories can increase the overall cost.

Choosing the Right Container for Sous Vide

When selecting a container or bath for Sous Vide, consider the following factors:

- **Size and Volume:** Choose a container that matches the amount of food you plan to cook.
- **Material:** Consider the durability, thermal insulation properties, and ease of care for the material.
- **Compatibility with Circulator:** Ensure the container fits your immersion circulator.
- **Additional Features:** Look for lids, insulation, and other accessories.

3.1.4. Vacuum Sealer Bags

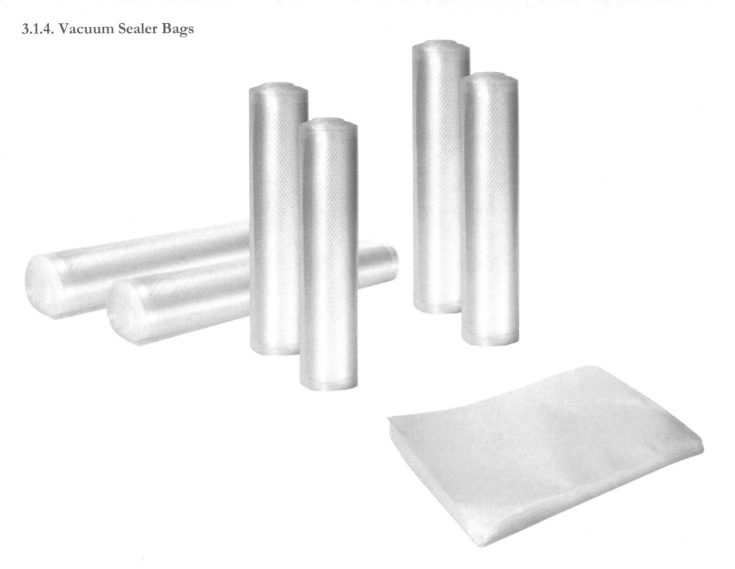

Vacuum sealer bags play a crucial role in the Sous Vide cooking process. They need to be durable, heat-resistant, and safe for food contact. There are several types of vacuum sealer bags, each with its own features and intended uses. Here are the main types of vacuum sealer bags and their characteristics:

1. Smooth Vacuum Bags These bags are typically used with chamber vacuum sealers.

- **Advantages:**
  - High strength and reliability.
  - Ability to package liquids and marinades.
  - Good airtightness.
- **Disadvantages:**
  - Require chamber sealers, which are more expensive and bulkier than external ones.

2. Embossed Vacuum Bags These bags have a textured surface that facilitates air removal and are often used with external vacuum sealers.

- **Advantages:**
  - Suitable for most household vacuum sealers.
  - Good airtightness.
  - Affordable price.
- **Disadvantages:**
  - Not always suitable for liquids (may require additional precautions).

3. Boilable Bags These bags are specifically designed to withstand high temperatures and can be used for Sous Vide cooking.

- **Advantages:**
    - o High heat resistance.
    - o Safe for use in boiling water.
    - o Suitable for freezing and subsequent cooking.
- **Disadvantages:**
    - o Can be more expensive than regular bags.

4. Reusable Vacuum Bags These bags can be used multiple times, making them more environmentally friendly.

- **Advantages:**
    - o Cost savings in the long run.
    - o Eco-friendly.
    - o Reusability.
- **Disadvantages:**
    - o Require careful maintenance and cleaning.
    - o May become less airtight over time.

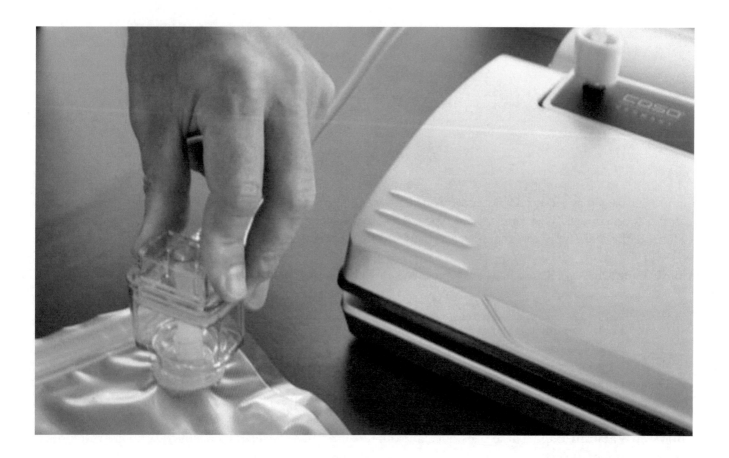

5. Liquid Block Bags These bags have special barriers to prevent liquids from leaking during vacuum sealing.

- **Advantages:**
    - o Convenient for packaging liquid products and marinades.
    - o Reliable airtightness.
- **Disadvantages:**

o   Higher cost.

6. Vacuum Seal Rolls These rolls allow you to create bags of the desired size by cutting the required length and sealing one end.

- **Advantages:**
    - o   Versatility.
    - o   Ability to create bags of any size.
    - o   Cost-effective.
- **Disadvantages:**
    - o   Requires extra time for sealing.

7. Valve Bags These bags are equipped with special valves for use with handheld vacuum sealers.

- **Advantages:**
    - o   Convenience of use.
    - o   Easy vacuuming.
- **Disadvantages:**
    - o   May be less durable compared to other types of bags.

Features and Usage

When choosing vacuum sealer bags, consider the following factors:

- **Material:** Bags should be made of high-quality materials that are safe for food contact and can withstand thermal processing.
- **Size:** Choose bags that are appropriately sized for the products you plan to cook or store.
- **Thickness:** Thicker bags are generally more durable and reliable but may be more expensive.
- **Compatibility with Sealer:** Ensure the selected bags are compatible with your vacuum sealer.

3.2. Additional Equipment

3.2.1. Thermometer for Accurate Temperature Measurement

While Sous Vide machines usually come with precise thermometers, an additional thermometer can be useful for monitoring the water and food temperatures. This is especially important when cooking temperature-sensitive products like meat or fish.

- **Advantages:**
  - Increased accuracy in temperature control.
  - Additional assurance of proper cooking.
  - Ability to check the calibration of the main thermometer.

3.2.2. Searing Tools

After cooking with Sous Vide, many dishes require a quick sear to create a delicious crust. For this, you will need:

- **Blowtorch:** Used for quick and even searing of the surface of foods without changing their internal temperature.
  - **Advantages:**
    - Fast and even crust creation.
    - Preservation of internal texture and juiciness.

- **Skillet:** A heavy cast iron or stainless steel skillet is perfect for searing foods after Sous Vide cooking.
  - **Advantages:**
    - High heat capacity and even heat distribution.
    - Versatility for various types of searing.

Using the right equipment will help you achieve the best results and enjoy delicious, healthy food cooked with the Sous Vide method.

3.2.3. Heat Retention Balls

Heat retention balls help reduce water evaporation and maintain a stable temperature in the container, which lowers energy consumption.

- **Advantages:**
  - Reduced water evaporation.
  - Maintained stable temperature.
  - Reduced energy consumption.
  - Easy to use and clean.

Insulate your heat
Reduce heat evaporation

3.2.4. Bag Racks

These accessories help keep bags with food in a vertical position, ensuring even cooking and improved water circulation.

- **Advantages:**
  - Even heat distribution.
  - Convenient placement of bags.
  - Reduced risk of obstructing water circulation.

Breakfasts

Oatmeal with Fruit

Ingredients:

- 1 cup rolled oats (240 ml)
- 2 cups almond milk (or other plant-based milk) (480 ml)
- 1 tablespoon chia seeds (15 ml)
- 1 tablespoon honey (optional) (15 ml)
- 1/2 cup chopped fresh fruit (berries, bananas, apples, kiwi) (120 ml)
- Pinch of cinnamon (optional)
- Pinch of salt

Instructions:

1. **Preparation:** In a large bowl, mix the rolled oats, almond milk, chia seeds, honey, cinnamon, and salt.
2. **Sealing:** Transfer the mixture to a vacuum-seal bag and seal it using a vacuum sealer.
3. **Sous Vide Cooking:** Preheat the Sous Vide water bath to 185°F (85°C). Place the vacuum-sealed bag with the oatmeal into the water and cook for 1 hour.
4. **Serving:** After cooking, remove the bag from the water and let it cool slightly. Open the bag and transfer the oatmeal to bowls. Top with fresh fruit before serving.

Cooking Time: 1 hour 10 minutes (including preparation and cooling time)
Servings: 2

Serving Tips:

- Oatmeal can be served warm or chilled.
- For additional flavor, sprinkle some nuts or coconut flakes on top.

Nutritional Information per Serving: Calories: 250, Protein: 8 g, Fat: 7 g, Carbohydrates: 38 g

Poached Eggs

Ingredients:

- 4 eggs
- 1 tablespoon white vinegar (15 ml)
- Salt and pepper to taste
- Chopped fresh herbs (e.g., green onions or dill) for garnish
- Toasted bread slices or English muffins for serving

Instructions:

1. **Prepare the Sous Vide Machine:** Preheat the Sous Vide water bath to 167°F (75°C).
2. **Prepare the Eggs:** Crack each egg into a small bowl or cup. Add a few drops of white vinegar to each cup with the egg.
3. **Sealing:** Carefully transfer the eggs into vacuum-seal bags, taking care not to break the yolks. Seal the bags using a vacuum sealer.
4. **Sous Vide Cooking:** Place the bags with the eggs into the Sous Vide machine and cook for 13 minutes.
5. **Final Preparation:** Remove the bags with the eggs from the water and carefully cut them open to extract the eggs. Season with salt and pepper to taste.
6. **Serving:** Serve the poached eggs on toasted bread slices or English muffins, garnished with fresh herbs.

Cooking Time: 20 minutes (including preparation and cooling time)
Servings: 2

Serving Tips:

- Serve poached eggs with avocado or fresh tomatoes for additional flavor and nutrients.
- If cooking for more people, increase the number of eggs and use multiple bags.
-

Nutritional Information per Serving: Calories: 150, Protein: 12 g, Fat: 10 g, Carbohydrates: 1 g

Ingredients:

- 1 liter whole milk (4 cups)
- 2 tablespoons natural yogurt (with live cultures) (30 ml)
- 1 tablespoon honey (optional) (15 ml)
- 1/2 cup fresh berries (strawberries, blueberries, raspberries) (120 ml)
- 1/4 cup nuts or granola for serving (60 ml)

Instructions:

1. **Prepare the milk:** Heat the milk in a saucepan to 185°F (85°C), then cool it to 109°F (43°C).
2. **Add yogurt:** In a bowl, mix the cooled milk with natural yogurt and honey (if using).
3. **Pour into jars:** Pour the mixture into glass jars and close them with lids.
4. **Sous Vide Cooking:** Preheat the Sous Vide water bath to 109°F (43°C). Place the jars with the yogurt mixture into the water and cook for 5-6 hours.
5. **Cooling:** Remove the jars from the water and chill in the refrigerator for at least 4 hours before serving.
6. **Serving:** Serve the yogurt in bowls, topped with fresh berries and nuts or granola.

Cooking Time: 6-7 hours (including cooking and cooling time)
Servings: 4-6

Serving Tips:

- You can serve yogurt with various types of berries and fruits of your choice.
- Store the yogurt in the refrigerator for up to one week.

Nutritional Information per Serving: Calories: 180, Protein: 8 g, Fat: 6 g, Carbohydrates: 20 g

Quinoa with Vegetables

Ingredients:

- 1 cup quinoa (240 ml)
- 2 cups vegetable broth or water (480 ml)
- 1 small zucchini, diced
- 1 small carrot, diced
- 1 red bell pepper, diced
- 1/2 cup frozen peas (120 ml)
- 2 tablespoons olive oil (30 ml)
- Salt and pepper to taste
- Juice of 1/2 lemon
- Fresh parsley for garnish

Instructions:

1. **Preparation:** Rinse the quinoa under cold water. In a bowl, mix the quinoa, vegetable broth or water, zucchini, carrot, red bell pepper, and peas.
2. **Sealing:** Transfer the mixture to a vacuum-seal bag and seal it using a vacuum sealer.
3. **Sous Vide Cooking:** Preheat the Sous Vide water bath to 194°F (90°C). Place the vacuum-sealed bag with the quinoa and vegetables into the water and cook for 1 hour.
4. **Serving:** After cooking, remove the bag from the water and carefully open it. Transfer the quinoa and vegetables to a bowl. Add the olive oil, lemon juice, salt, and pepper to taste, and mix well. Garnish with fresh parsley before serving.

Cooking Time: 1 hour 15 minutes (including preparation and cooling time)
Servings: 2-3

Serving Tips:

- Serve the quinoa and vegetables either hot or cold.
- Add some toasted nuts or seeds for extra texture.

Nutritional Information per Serving: Calories: 250, Protein: 8 g, Fat: 10 g, Carbohydrates: 35 g.

Apple Oat Pancakes

Ingredients:

- 1 cup rolled oats (240 ml)
- 1 cup milk (or plant-based milk) (240 ml)
- 1 apple, grated
- 2 eggs
- 1 tablespoon honey (15 ml)
- 1 teaspoon cinnamon (5 ml)
- 1 teaspoon baking powder (5 ml)
- Pinch of salt
- 1 tablespoon olive oil for frying (15 ml)

Instructions:

1. **Prepare the Batter:** In a bowl, mix the rolled oats, milk, grated apple, eggs, honey, cinnamon, baking powder, and salt until well combined.
2. **Sealing:** Transfer the mixture to a vacuum-seal bag and seal it using a vacuum sealer.
3. **Sous Vide Cooking:** Preheat the Sous Vide water bath to 185°F (85°C). Place the vacuum-sealed bag with the batter into the water and cook for 1 hour.
4. **Frying:** After cooking, remove the bag from the water and carefully open it. Spoon small portions of the batter onto a skillet with heated olive oil and fry the pancakes until golden brown on both sides.
5. **Serving:** Serve the pancakes with honey, yogurt, or fresh fruits to taste.

Cooking Time: 1 hour 20 minutes (including preparation and frying time)
Servings: 4-6

Serving Tips:

- Serve the pancakes with honey, yogurt, or fresh fruits for extra flavor.
- Add some nuts or seeds for texture.

Nutritional Information per Serving: Calories: 250, Protein: 8 g, Fat: 10 g, Carbohydrates: 35 g

Protein Banana Pancakes

Ingredients:

- 1 cup oat flour (240 ml)
- 1 ripe banana, mashed
- 1/2 cup egg whites (about 4 whites) (120 ml)
- 1/2 cup Greek yogurt (120 ml)
- 1 teaspoon vanilla extract (5 ml)
- 1 teaspoon baking powder (5 ml)
- Pinch of salt
- 1 tablespoon coconut oil for frying (15 ml)

Instructions:

1. **Prepare the Batter:** In a bowl, mix the oat flour, baking powder, and salt. In another bowl, combine the mashed banana, egg whites, Greek yogurt, and vanilla extract. Combine the dry and wet ingredients, stirring until smooth.
2. **Sealing:** Transfer the mixture to a vacuum-seal bag and seal it using a vacuum sealer.
3. **Sous Vide Cooking:** Preheat the Sous Vide water bath to 167°F (75°C). Place the vacuum-sealed bag with the batter into the water and cook for 1 hour.
4. **Frying:** After cooking, remove the bag from the water and carefully open it. Spoon small portions of the batter onto a skillet with heated coconut oil and fry the pancakes until golden brown on both sides.
5. **Serving:** Serve the protein banana pancakes with honey, yogurt, or fresh fruits to taste.

Cooking Time: 1 hour 20 minutes (including preparation and frying time)
Servings: 4-6

Serving Tips:
- Serve the pancakes with honey, yogurt, or fresh fruits for extra flavor.
- Add some nuts or seeds for texture.

Nutritional Information per Serving: Calories: 200, Protein: 12 g, Fat: 6 g, Carbohydrates: 28 g

Ingredients:

- 4 eggs
- 1/4 cup milk (or plant-based milk) (60 ml)
- 1 small tomato, diced
- 1/4 cup diced bell pepper (60 ml)
- 1/4 cup diced zucchini (60 ml)
- 1/4 cup chopped spinach (60 ml)

- 2 tablespoons grated cheese (optional) (30 ml)
- Salt and pepper to taste
- Fresh herbs for garnish (e.g., parsley or green onions)

Instructions:

1. **Prepare the Egg Mixture:** In a bowl, whisk the eggs with milk, salt, and pepper until smooth. Add the diced vegetables and grated cheese (if using), and mix well.
2. **Sealing:** Transfer the egg mixture to a vacuum-seal bag and seal it using a vacuum sealer.
3. **Sous Vide Cooking:** Preheat the Sous Vide water bath to 167°F (75°C). Place the vacuum-sealed bag with the egg mixture into the water and cook for 45 minutes.
4. **Serving:** After cooking, remove the bag from the water and carefully open it. Transfer the omelet to a plate and garnish with fresh herbs before serving.

Cooking Time: 1 hour (including preparation and cooling time)
Servings: 2-3

Serving Tips:

- Serve the omelet with toasted bread slices or English muffins.
- For extra flavor, add a bit of hot sauce or avocado.

Nutritional Information per Serving: Calories: 180, Protein: 12 g, Fat: 12 g, Carbohydrates: 6 g

Protein Avocado Smoothie

Ingredients:

- 1 ripe avocado
- 1 banana
- 1 cup spinach (240 ml)
- 1/2 cup Greek yogurt (120 ml)
- 1/2 cup almond milk (or other plant-based milk) (120 ml)
- 1 scoop vanilla protein powder
- 1 tablespoon honey (optional) (15 ml)
- 1/2 cup ice (120 ml)

Instructions:

1. **Prepare the Ingredients:** Peel the avocado and banana. Cut the avocado into pieces.
2. **Sealing:** Vacuum-seal the avocado, banana, and spinach in a bag using a vacuum sealer.
3. **Sous Vide Cooking:** Preheat the Sous Vide water bath to 185°F (85°C). Place the vacuum-sealed bag with the ingredients into the water and cook for 30 minutes.
4. **Blending:** After cooking, remove the bag from the water and let the ingredients cool. In a blender, combine the cooked ingredients with Greek yogurt, almond milk, protein powder, honey (if using), and ice. Blend until smooth.
5. **Serving:** Pour the smoothie into glasses and serve immediately.

Cooking Time: 40 minutes (including preparation and cooling time)
Servings: 2

Serving Tips:

- Serve the smoothie immediately to retain freshness and nutrients.
- Garnish the smoothie with a few chia seeds or a slice of avocado for a decorative touch.

Nutritional Information per Serving: Calories: 250, Protein: 12 g, Fat: 10 g, Carbohydrates: 30 g

Cottage Cheese Pancakes

Ingredients:

- 500 g cottage cheese (preferably 5-9% fat) (about 2 cups)
- 2 eggs
- 3 tablespoons flour (45 ml)
- 2 tablespoons sugar (30 ml)
- 1 teaspoon vanilla extract (5 ml)
- Pinch of salt
- 1 tablespoon vegetable oil for frying (15 ml)

Instructions:

1. **Prepare the Batter:** In a bowl, mix the cottage cheese, eggs, flour, sugar, vanilla extract, and salt until smooth. Form small patties from the mixture.
2. **Sealing:** Vacuum-seal the patties in bags using a vacuum sealer.
3. **Sous Vide Cooking:** Preheat the Sous Vide water bath to 167°F (75°C). Place the vacuum-sealed bags with the patties into the water and cook for 1 hour.
4. **Frying:** After cooking, remove the bags from the water and carefully open them. Heat a skillet with vegetable oil and fry the syrniki until golden brown on both sides.
5. **Serving:** Serve the syrniki with honey, sour cream, or fresh berries to taste.

Cooking Time: 1 hour 20 minutes (including preparation and frying time)
Servings: 4-6

Serving Tips:
- Serve the syrniki with honey, sour cream, or fresh berries for extra flavor.
- Add a bit of cinnamon or lemon zest for aroma.

Nutritional Information per Serving: Calories: 200, Protein: 12 g, Fat: 10 g, Carbohydrates: 18 g

Almond Milk with Muesli

Ingredients:

- 1 cup almonds (240 ml)
- 4 cups water (960 ml)
- 1 tablespoon honey or maple syrup (15 ml)
- 1 teaspoon vanilla extract (5 ml)
- Pinch of salt
- 1 cup muesli (240 ml)
- Fresh fruits and berries for serving

Instructions:

1. **Soaking the Almonds:** Soak the almonds in water overnight or for at least 8 hours.
2. **Preparing Almond Milk:** Drain and rinse the almonds. In a blender, combine the almonds with 4 cups of fresh water, honey, vanilla extract, and salt. Blend until smooth. Strain the mixture through cheesecloth or a nut milk bag.
3. **Sous Vide Cooking:** Preheat the Sous Vide water bath to 185°F (85°C). Transfer the almond milk to a vacuum-seal bag and seal it using a vacuum sealer. Place the bag with the milk into the water and cook for 30 minutes.
4. **Cooling:** Remove the bag from the water and let the milk cool. Transfer the milk to a bottle and store it in the refrigerator.
5. **Serving:** Serve the almond milk with muesli, fresh fruits, and berries.

Cooking Time: 9 hours (including soaking and cooking time)
Servings: 4

Serving Tips:
- You can substitute muesli with granola or oatmeal according to your taste.
- The milk can be used for 3-4 days when stored in the refrigerator.

Nutritional Information per Serving: Calories: 150, Protein: 5 g, Fat: 8 g, Carbohydrates: 18 g

Chicken Breast with Vegetables

Ingredients:

- 2 chicken breasts (about 500 g or 1 lb)
- 1 cup chopped broccoli (240 ml)
- 1 cup chopped carrots (240 ml)
- 1 red bell pepper, sliced
- 2 tablespoons olive oil (30 ml)
- 1 teaspoon dried thyme (5 ml)
- 1 teaspoon dried rosemary (5 ml)
- Salt and pepper to taste
- Juice of 1/2 lemon

Instructions:

1. **Prepare the Chicken:** Season the chicken breasts with salt, pepper, dried thyme, and rosemary. Add a bit of lemon juice.
2. **Prepare the Vegetables:** In a bowl, mix the broccoli, carrots, and red bell pepper with olive oil, salt, and pepper.
3. **Sealing:** Vacuum-seal the chicken breasts in one bag and the vegetables in another bag using a vacuum sealer.
4. **Sous Vide Cooking:** Preheat the Sous Vide water bath to 149°F (65°C). Place the bags with the chicken and vegetables into the water and cook for 1 hour.
5. **Final Preparation:** Remove the bags from the water and carefully open them. Sear the chicken breasts in a skillet with a small amount of olive oil until golden brown.
6. **Serving:** Serve the chicken breasts with the vegetables, garnished with fresh herbs and a bit of lemon juice to taste.

Cooking Time: 1 hour 20 minutes (including preparation and searing time)

Servings: 2

Serving Tips:

- Serve the chicken with vegetables and a side of quinoa or brown rice for extra nutrition.
- Add garlic and onions for a richer flavor.

Nutritional Information per Serving: Calories: 350, Protein: 30 g, Fat: 15 g, Carbohydrates: 25 g

Salmon with Asparagus

Ingredients:

- 2 salmon fillets (about 400 g or 14 oz)
- 1 bunch asparagus
- 2 tablespoons olive oil (30 ml)
- 1 tablespoon lemon juice (15 ml)
- 1 teaspoon lemon zest (5 ml)
- Salt and pepper to taste
- Fresh dill for garnish

Instructions:

1. **Prepare the Salmon:** Season the salmon fillets with salt, pepper, lemon zest, and lemon juice.
2. **Prepare the Asparagus:** Trim the ends of the asparagus and toss with 1 tablespoon of olive oil, salt, and pepper.
3. **Sealing:** Vacuum-seal the salmon in one bag and the asparagus in another bag using a vacuum sealer.
4. **Sous Vide Cooking:** Preheat the Sous Vide water bath to 122°F (50°C). Place the bags with the salmon and asparagus into the water and cook for 45 minutes.
5. **Final Preparation:** Remove the bags from the water and carefully open them. Sear the salmon in a skillet with the remaining olive oil until golden brown.
6. **Serving:** Serve the salmon with the asparagus, garnished with fresh dill and a bit of lemon juice to taste.

Cooking Time: 1 hour (including preparation and searing time)
Servings: 2

Serving Tips:

- Serve the salmon with a side of wild rice or quinoa for extra nutrition.
- Add a bit of butter to the salmon before serving for a richer flavor.

Nutritional Information per Serving: Calories: 300, Protein: 25 g, Fat: 20 g, Carbohydrates: 5 g

Rosemary Beef Steak

Ingredients:

- 2 beef steaks (about 400 g or 14 oz each)
- 2 tablespoons olive oil (30 ml)
- 2 sprigs fresh rosemary
- 2 garlic cloves, crushed
- Salt and pepper to taste
- 1 tablespoon butter (15 ml)

Instructions:

1. **Prepare the Steaks:** Season the steaks with salt and pepper on both sides.
2. **Sealing:** Vacuum-seal the steaks in bags, adding a sprig of rosemary and a garlic clove to each bag. Seal the bags using a vacuum sealer.
3. **Sous Vide Cooking:** Preheat the Sous Vide water bath to 133°F (56°C) for medium-rare. Place the bags with the steaks into the water and cook for 1.5 hours.
4. **Final Preparation:** Remove the bags from the water and carefully open them. Heat a skillet with olive oil and butter over high heat. Sear the steaks on each side until golden brown, about 1-2 minutes per side.
5. **Serving:** Serve the steaks with your favorite side dish, garnished with fresh herbs.

Cooking Time: 1 hour 45 minutes (including preparation and searing time)
Servings: 2

Serving Tips:

- Serve the steaks with a side of roasted vegetables or mashed potatoes.
- For a richer flavor, add a splash of red wine to the skillet while searing the steaks.

Nutritional Information per Serving: Calories: 400, Protein: 30 g, Fat: 28 g, Carbohydrates: 2 g

Rosemary Turkey

Ingredients:

- 2 turkey fillets (about 400 g or 14 oz each)
- 2 tablespoons olive oil (30 ml)
- 2 sprigs fresh rosemary
- 2 garlic cloves, crushed
- Salt and pepper to taste
- Juice of 1/2 lemon

Instructions:

1. **Prepare the Turkey:** Season the turkey fillets with salt, pepper, and lemon juice on both sides.
2. **Sealing:** Vacuum-seal the turkey fillets in bags, adding a sprig of rosemary and a garlic clove to each bag. Seal the bags using a vacuum sealer.
3. **Sous Vide Cooking:** Preheat the Sous Vide water bath to 149°F (65°C). Place the bags with the turkey into the water and cook for 2 hours.
4. **Final Preparation:** Remove the bags from the water and carefully open them. Heat a skillet with olive oil over high heat. Sear the turkey fillets on each side until golden brown, about 1-2 minutes per side.
5. **Serving:** Serve the turkey with your favorite side dish, garnished with fresh herbs.

Cooking Time: 2 hours 20 minutes (including preparation and searing time)
Servings: 2

Serving Tips:

- Serve the turkey with a side of roasted vegetables or mashed potatoes.
- For a richer flavor, add a splash of white wine to the skillet while searing the turkey fillets.

Nutritional Information per Serving: Calories: 350, Protein: 30 g, Fat: 20 g, Carbohydrates: 2 g

Pork with Apples and Cinnamon

Ingredients:

- 2 pork chops (about 400 g or 14 oz each)
- 2 apples, sliced
- 2 tablespoons brown sugar (30 ml)
- 1 teaspoon ground cinnamon (5 ml)

- 2 tablespoons olive oil (30 ml)
- Salt and pepper to taste
- 1 tablespoon butter (15 ml)

Instructions:

1. **Prepare the Pork:** Season the pork chops with salt and pepper on both sides.
2. **Prepare the Apples:** In a bowl, mix the apple slices with brown sugar and cinnamon.
3. **Sealing:** Vacuum-seal the pork chops in one bag and the apples in another bag using a vacuum sealer.
4. **Sous Vide Cooking:** Preheat the Sous Vide water bath to 140°F (60°C). Place the bags with the pork and apples into the water and cook for 1.5 hours.
5. **Final Preparation:** Remove the bags from the water and carefully open them. Heat a skillet with olive oil and butter over high heat. Sear the pork on each side until golden brown, about 1-2 minutes per side. Remove the pork and quickly sauté the apples until soft.
6. **Serving:** Serve the pork with the apples, garnished with fresh herbs.

Cooking Time: 1 hour 45 minutes (including preparation and searing time)
Servings: 2

Serving Tips:

- Serve the pork with a side of mashed potatoes or roasted vegetables.
- Add a splash of apple cider to the skillet while sautéing for a richer flavor.

Nutritional Information per Serving: Calories: 450, Protein: 30 g, Fat: 25 g, Carbohydrates: 30 g

Filet Mignon

Ingredients:

- 2 filet mignon steaks (about 200 g or 7 oz each)
- 2 tablespoons olive oil (30 ml)
- 2 garlic cloves, crushed
- 2 sprigs fresh thyme
- Salt and pepper to taste
- 1 tablespoon butter (15 ml)

Instructions:

1. **Prepare the Steaks:** Season the filet mignon steaks with salt and pepper on both sides.
2. **Sealing:** Vacuum-seal the steaks in bags, adding a crushed garlic clove and a sprig of thyme to each bag. Seal the bags using a vacuum sealer.
3. **Sous Vide Cooking:** Preheat the Sous Vide water bath to 129°F (54°C) for medium-rare. Place the bags with the steaks into the water and cook for 1.5 hours.
4. **Final Preparation:** Remove the bags from the water and carefully open them. Heat a skillet with olive oil and butter over high heat. Sear the steaks on each side until golden brown, about 1-2 minutes per side.
5. **Serving:** Serve the filet mignon steaks with your favorite side dish, garnished with fresh herbs.

Cooking Time: 1 hour 45 minutes (including preparation and searing time)
Servings: 2

Serving Tips:

- Serve the steaks with a side of roasted vegetables or mashed potatoes.
- For a richer flavor, add a splash of red wine to the skillet while searing the steaks.

Nutritional Information per Serving: Calories: 450, Protein: 40 g, Fat: 30 g, Carbohydrates: 2 g

Cod with Lemon and Dill

Ingredients:

- 2 cod fillets (about 200 g or 7 oz each)
- 1 lemon, thinly sliced
- 2 tablespoons olive oil (30 ml)
- 2 sprigs fresh dill
- Salt and pepper to taste

Instructions:

1. **Prepare the Cod:** Season the cod fillets with salt and pepper on both sides.
2. **Sealing:** Vacuum-seal the cod fillets in bags, adding a few lemon slices and a sprig of dill to each bag. Seal the bags using a vacuum sealer.
3. **Sous Vide Cooking:** Preheat the Sous Vide water bath to 131°F (55°C). Place the bags with the cod into the water and cook for 45 minutes.
4. **Final Preparation:** Remove the bags from the water and carefully open them. Heat a skillet with olive oil over medium heat. Sear the cod on each side until golden brown, about 1-2 minutes per side.
5. **Serving:** Serve the cod with a side of fresh vegetables, garnished with lemon slices and fresh dill.

Cooking Time: 1 hour (including preparation and searing time)
Servings: 2

Serving Tips:

- Serve the cod with a side of quinoa or rice for extra nutrition.
- Add a splash of white wine to the skillet while searing for a richer flavor.

Nutritional Information per Serving: Calories: 250, Protein: 25 g, Fat: 15 g, Carbohydrates: 3 g

Teriyaki Chicken

Ingredients:

- 2 boneless, skinless chicken thighs (about 400 g or 14 oz)
- 1/2 cup teriyaki sauce (120 ml)
- 2 tablespoons soy sauce (30 ml)
- 1 tablespoon honey (15 ml)
- 2 garlic cloves, minced
- 1 teaspoon freshly grated ginger (5 ml)
- 1 tablespoon sesame oil (15 ml)
- Salt and pepper to taste
- Chopped green onions and sesame seeds for garnish

Instructions:

Prepare the Marinade: In a bowl, mix the teriyaki sauce, soy sauce, honey, minced garlic, grated ginger, and sesame oil.

Marinate the Chicken: Place the chicken thighs in a vacuum-seal bag and pour in the marinade. Vacuum-seal the bag using a vacuum sealer and let it marinate in the refrigerator for 1 hour.

Sous Vide Cooking: Preheat the Sous Vide water bath to 149°F (65°C). Place the bag with the chicken thighs into the water and cook for 1.5 hours.

Final Preparation: Remove the bag from the water and carefully open it. Heat a skillet over medium heat and sear the chicken thighs until golden brown, about 1-2 minutes per side.

Serving: Serve the teriyaki chicken with a side of rice or vegetables, garnished with chopped green onions and sesame seeds.

Cooking Time: 2 hours 30 minutes (including marinating, cooking, and searing time)
Servings: 2

Serving Tips:

- Serve the chicken with a side of rice or stir-fried vegetables.
- For a richer flavor, add a bit of the marinade to the skillet while searing.

Nutritional Information per Serving: Calories: 350, Protein: 30 g, Fat: 15 g, Carbohydrates: 25 g

Garlic and Rosemary Lamb Chops

Ingredients:

- 4 lamb chops (about 800 g or 28 oz)
- 4 garlic cloves, crushed
- 2 sprigs fresh rosemary
- 2 tablespoons olive oil (30 ml)
- Salt and pepper to taste

Instructions:

1. **Prepare the Chops:** Season the lamb chops with salt and pepper on both sides.
2. **Sealing:** Vacuum-seal the chops in bags, adding a crushed garlic clove and a sprig of rosemary to each bag. Seal the bags using a vacuum sealer.
3. **Sous Vide Cooking:** Preheat the Sous Vide water bath to 135°F (57°C). Place the bags with the chops into the water and cook for 4 hours.
4. **Final Preparation:** Remove the bags from the water and carefully open them. Heat a skillet with olive oil over high heat. Sear the chops on each side until golden brown, about 1-2 minutes per side.
5. **Serving:** Serve the lamb chops with your favorite side dish, garnished with fresh herbs.

Cooking Time: 4 hours 20 minutes (including preparation and searing time)
Servings: 2

Serving Tips:
- Serve the chops with a side of roasted vegetables or mashed potatoes.
- For a richer flavor, add a splash of red wine to the skillet while searing the chops.

Nutritional Information per Serving: Calories: 500, Protein: 40 g, Fat: 35 g, Carbohydrates: 2 g

Garlic and Lemon Shrimp

Ingredients:

- 500 g peeled shrimp (1 lb)
- 3 garlic cloves, minced
- Juice of 1 lemon
- Zest of 1 lemon
- 2 tablespoons olive oil (30 ml)
- Salt and pepper to taste
- Fresh parsley for garnish

Instructions:

1. **Prepare the Shrimp:** In a bowl, mix the shrimp with minced garlic, lemon juice, lemon zest, olive oil, salt, and pepper.
2. **Sealing:** Vacuum-seal the shrimp in a bag using a vacuum sealer.
3. **Sous Vide Cooking:** Preheat the Sous Vide water bath to 140°F (60°C). Place the bag with the shrimp into the water and cook for 30 minutes.
4. **Final Preparation:** Remove the bag from the water and carefully open it. Sear the shrimp in a skillet over medium heat until lightly golden, about 1-2 minutes.
5. **Serving:** Serve the shrimp with a side of rice or vegetables, garnished with fresh parsley.

Cooking Time: 45 minutes (including preparation and searing time)
Servings: 2-3

Serving Tips:

- Serve the shrimp with a side of rice or sautéed vegetables.
- For a richer flavor, add a splash of white wine to the skillet while searing the shrimp.

Nutritional Information per Serving: Calories: 200, Protein: 24 g, Fat: 10 g, Carbohydrates: 3 g

Duck with Oranges

Ingredients:

- 2 duck breasts (about 400 g or 14 oz each)
- 1 orange, thinly sliced
- Juice of 1 orange
- 2 tablespoons honey (30 ml)

- 2 garlic cloves, crushed
- 2 sprigs fresh thyme
- Salt and pepper to taste

Instructions:

1. **Prepare the Duck:** Season the duck breasts with salt and pepper on both sides.
2. **Sealing:** Vacuum-seal the duck breasts in bags, adding orange slices, orange juice, honey, crushed garlic, and a sprig of thyme to each bag. Seal the bags using a vacuum sealer.
3. **Sous Vide Cooking:** Preheat the Sous Vide water bath to 136°F (58°C). Place the bags with the duck into the water and cook for 2 hours.
4. **Final Preparation:** Remove the bags from the water and carefully open them. Heat a skillet over medium heat. Sear the duck breasts skin-side down until golden brown, about 2-3 minutes on each side.
5. **Serving:** Serve the duck breasts with the oranges, garnished with fresh herbs.

Cooking Time: 2 hours 20 minutes (including preparation and searing time)
Servings: 2

Serving Tips:

- Serve the duck with a side of mashed potatoes or roasted vegetables.
- For a richer flavor, add a splash of orange liqueur to the skillet while searing the duck.

Nutritional Information per Serving: Calories: 450, Protein: 30 g, Fat: 25 g, Carbohydrates: 20 g

Halibut with Tomatoes and Basil

Ingredients:

- 2 halibut fillets (about 200 g or 7 oz each)
- 2 ripe tomatoes, diced
- 2 tablespoons olive oil (30 ml)
- 1 tablespoon lemon juice (15 ml)
- 2 garlic cloves, minced
- 2 tablespoons fresh basil, chopped (30 ml)
- Salt and pepper to taste

Instructions:

1. **Prepare the Halibut:** Season the halibut fillets with salt and pepper on both sides.
2. **Sealing:** Vacuum-seal the halibut fillets in bags, adding diced tomatoes, minced garlic, olive oil, and lemon juice to each bag. Seal the bags using a vacuum sealer.
3. **Sous Vide Cooking:** Preheat the Sous Vide water bath to 131°F (55°C). Place the bags with the halibut into the water and cook for 45 minutes.
4. **Final Preparation:** Remove the bags from the water and carefully open them. Heat a skillet over medium heat and sear the halibut fillets until lightly golden, about 1-2 minutes per side.
5. **Serving:** Serve the halibut with tomatoes and basil, garnished with fresh herbs.

Cooking Time: 1 hour (including preparation and searing time)
Servings: 2

Serving Tips:

- Serve the halibut with a side of rice or quinoa.
- For a richer flavor, add a splash of white wine to the skillet while searing the fish.

Nutritional Information per Serving: Calories: 300, Protein: 25 g, Fat: 15 g, Carbohydrates: 5 g

Vegetable Stew with Tofu

Ingredients:

- 200 g firm tofu, cubed (7 oz)
- 1 small zucchini, cubed
- 1 red bell pepper, sliced
- 1 small carrot, cubed
- 1 cup broccoli florets (240 ml)
- 1 onion, sliced into half-moons
- 2 garlic cloves, minced
- 2 tablespoons soy sauce (30 ml)
- 1 tablespoon olive oil (15 ml)
- 1 teaspoon dried thyme (5 ml)
- Salt and pepper to taste

Instructions:

1. **Prepare the Ingredients:** In a bowl, mix all the chopped vegetables, tofu, minced garlic, soy sauce, olive oil, thyme, salt, and pepper.
2. **Sealing:** Transfer the mixture to a vacuum-seal bag and seal it using a vacuum sealer.
3. **Sous Vide Cooking:** Preheat the Sous Vide water bath to 185°F (85°C). Place the bag with the vegetable mixture into the water and cook for 1 hour.
4. **Final Preparation:** Remove the bag from the water and carefully open it. Transfer the vegetable stew with tofu to plates.
5. **Serving:** Serve the vegetable stew with a side of rice or quinoa, garnished with fresh herbs.

Cooking Time: 1 hour 20 minutes (including preparation and cooling time)
Servings: 2-3

Serving Tips:
- Serve the vegetable stew with a side of rice, quinoa, or bulgur for added nutrition.
- Add a bit of fresh lemon juice before serving for a refreshing taste.

Nutritional Information per Serving: Calories: 250, Protein: 10 g, Fat: 10 g, Carbohydrates: 30 g

Tandoori Chicken

Ingredients:

- 2 skinless, boneless chicken thighs (about 400 g or 14 oz)
- 1/2 cup yogurt (120 ml)
- 2 tablespoons lemon juice (30 ml)
- 2 tablespoons tandoori paste (30 ml)
- 2 garlic cloves, minced
- 1 tablespoon fresh ginger, grated (15 ml)
- 1 teaspoon ground turmeric (5 ml)
- 1 teaspoon ground cumin (5 ml)
- Salt and pepper to taste
- Fresh cilantro for garnish

Instructions:

1. Prepare the Marinade: In a bowl, mix yogurt, lemon juice, tandoori paste, minced garlic, grated ginger, ground turmeric, ground cumin, salt, and pepper.
2. Marinate the Chicken: Place the chicken thighs in a vacuum-seal bag and pour the marinade over them. Vacuum-seal the bag using a vacuum sealer and refrigerate for 1 hour.
3. Sous Vide Cooking: Preheat the Sous Vide water bath to 149°F (65°C). Place the bag with the chicken thighs into the water and cook for 1.5 hours.
4. Final Preparation: Remove the bag from the water and carefully open it. Heat a skillet over medium heat and sear the chicken thighs until golden brown, about 1-2 minutes per side.
5. Serving: Serve the tandoori chicken with a side of rice or vegetables, garnished with fresh cilantro.

Cooking Time: 2 hours 30 minutes (including marinating, cooking, and searing time)
Servings: 2

Serving Tips:

- Serve the chicken with a side of basmati rice and naan.
- For additional flavor, add a splash of fresh lemon juice before serving.

Nutritional Information per Serving: Calories: 350, Protein: 30 g, Fat: 15 g, Carbohydrates: 20 g

Sea Bass with Lemon and Herbs

Ingredients:

- 2 sea bass fillets (about 200 g or 7 oz each)
- 1 lemon, thinly sliced
- 2 tablespoons olive oil (30 ml)
- 2 sprigs fresh thyme
- 2 garlic cloves, crushed
- Salt and pepper to taste
- Fresh parsley for garnish

Instructions:

1. **Prepare the Sea Bass:** Season the sea bass fillets with salt and pepper on both sides.
2. **Sealing:** Vacuum-seal the sea bass fillets in bags, adding a few lemon slices, crushed garlic, and a sprig of thyme to each bag. Seal the bags using a vacuum sealer.
3. **Sous Vide Cooking:** Preheat the Sous Vide water bath to 131°F (55°C). Place the bags with the sea bass into the water and cook for 45 minutes.
4. **Final Preparation:** Remove the bags from the water and carefully open them. Heat a skillet with olive oil over medium heat. Sear the sea bass fillets until lightly golden, about 1-2 minutes per side.
5. **Serving:** Serve the sea bass with a side of fresh vegetables, garnished with lemon slices and fresh parsley.

Cooking Time: 1 hour (including preparation and searing time)
Servings: 2

Serving Tips:

- Serve the sea bass with a side of rice or quinoa.
- For enhanced flavor, add a splash of white wine to the skillet during the searing process.

Nutritional Information per Serving: Calories: 250, Protein: 25 g, Fat: 15 g, Carbohydrates: 3 g

Garlic Pork Chops

Ingredients:

- 2 pork chops (about 400 g or 14 oz each)
- 3 garlic cloves, crushed
- 2 tablespoons olive oil (30 ml)
- 2 sprigs fresh thyme
- Salt and pepper to taste
- 1 tablespoon butter (15 g)

Instructions:

1. **Prepare the Pork Chops:** Season the pork chops with salt and pepper on both sides.
2. **Sealing:** Vacuum-seal the pork chops in bags, adding crushed garlic and a sprig of thyme to each bag. Seal the bags using a vacuum sealer.
3. **Sous Vide Cooking:** Preheat the Sous Vide water bath to 140°F (60°C). Place the bags with the pork chops into the water and cook for 2 hours.
4. **Final Preparation:** Remove the bags from the water and carefully open them. Heat a skillet with olive oil and butter over high heat. Sear the pork chops until golden brown, about 1-2 minutes per side.
5. **Serving:** Serve the pork chops with your favorite side dish, garnished with fresh herbs.

Cooking Time: 2 hours 20 minutes (including preparation and searing time)
Servings: 2

Serving Tips:

- Serve the pork chops with mashed potatoes or roasted vegetables.
- For enhanced flavor, add a splash of white wine to the skillet during searing.

Nutritional Information per Serving: Calories: 400, Protein: 35 g, Fat: 25 g, Carbohydrates: 2 g

Lemon Garlic Tilapia

Ingredients:

- 2 tilapia fillets (about 200 g or 7 oz each)
- 2 garlic cloves, minced
- Juice of 1 lemon
- Zest of 1 lemon
- 2 tablespoons olive oil (30 ml)
- Salt and pepper to taste
- Fresh dill for garnish

Instructions:

1. **Prepare the Tilapia:** Season the tilapia fillets with salt and pepper on both sides.
2. **Sealing:** Vacuum-seal the tilapia fillets in bags, adding minced garlic, lemon juice, lemon zest, and olive oil to each bag. Seal the bags using a vacuum sealer.
3. **Sous Vide Cooking:** Preheat the Sous Vide water bath to 131°F (55°C). Place the bags with the tilapia into the water and cook for 45 minutes.
4. **Final Preparation:** Remove the bags from the water and carefully open them. Heat a skillet over medium heat and sear the tilapia fillets until lightly golden, about 1-2 minutes per side.
5. **Serving:** Serve the tilapia with a side of fresh vegetables or rice, garnished with fresh dill.

Cooking Time: 1 hour (including preparation and searing time)
Servings: 2

Serving Tips:

- Serve the tilapia with a side of rice or quinoa for added nutrition.
- For enhanced flavor, add a splash of white wine to the skillet during searing.

Nutritional Information per Serving: Calories: 250, Protein: 25 g, Fat: 12 g, Carbohydrates: 3 g

Lemon Garlic Chicken Thighs

Ingredients:

- 4 boneless, skinless chicken thighs (about 500 g or 1.1 lbs)
- 3 garlic cloves, minced
- Juice of 1 lemon
- Zest of 1 lemon
- 2 tablespoons olive oil (30 ml)
- Salt and pepper to taste
- Fresh thyme for garnish

Instructions:

1. **Prepare the Chicken Thighs:** Season the chicken thighs with salt and pepper on both sides.
2. **Sealing:** Vacuum-seal the chicken thighs in bags, adding minced garlic, lemon juice, lemon zest, and olive oil to each bag. Seal the bags using a vacuum sealer.
3. **Sous Vide Cooking:** Preheat the Sous Vide water bath to 149°F (65°C). Place the bags with the chicken thighs into the water and cook for 1.5 hours.
4. **Final Preparation:** Remove the bags from the water and carefully open them. Heat a skillet over medium heat and sear the chicken thighs until golden brown, about 1-2 minutes per side.
5. **Serving:** Serve the chicken thighs with a side of fresh vegetables or rice, garnished with fresh thyme.

Cooking Time: 2 hours (including preparation and searing time)
Servings: 2-3

Serving Tips:

- Serve the chicken thighs with a side of rice or mashed potatoes for added nutrition.
- For enhanced flavor, add a splash of white wine to the skillet during searing.

Nutritional Information per Serving: Calories: 300, Protein: 25 g, Fat: 15 g, Carbohydrates: 5 g

Lemon Garlic Tuna Fillets

Ingredients:

- 2 tuna fillets (about 200 g or 7 oz each)
- 2 garlic cloves, minced
- Juice of 1 lemon
- Zest of 1 lemon
- 2 tablespoons olive oil (30 ml)
- Salt and pepper to taste
- Fresh basil for garnish

Instructions:

1. **Prepare the Tuna:** Season the tuna fillets with salt and pepper on both sides.
2. **Sealing:** Vacuum-seal the tuna fillets in bags, adding minced garlic, lemon juice, lemon zest, and olive oil to each bag. Seal the bags using a vacuum sealer.
3. **Sous Vide Cooking:** Preheat the Sous Vide water bath to 129°F (54°C). Place the bags with the tuna into the water and cook for 45 minutes.
4. **Final Preparation:** Remove the bags from the water and carefully open them. Heat a skillet over medium heat and sear the tuna fillets until lightly golden, about 1 minute on each side.
5. **Serving:** Serve the tuna with a side of fresh vegetables or rice, garnished with fresh basil.

Cooking Time: 1 hour (including preparation and searing time)
Servings: 2

Serving Tips:

- Serve the tuna with a side of rice or quinoa for added nutrition.
- For enhanced flavor, add a splash of white wine to the skillet during searing.

Nutritional Information per Serving: Calories: 250, Protein: 30 g, Fat: 12 g, Carbohydrates: 2 g

Herb-Roasted Turkey

Ingredients:

- 2 turkey fillets (about 400 g or 14 oz each)
- 3 garlic cloves, minced
- 2 tablespoons olive oil (30 ml)
- 1 tablespoon butter (15 ml)
- 2 sprigs fresh thyme
- 2 sprigs fresh rosemary
- Salt and pepper to taste
- Juice of 1/2 lemon

Instructions:

1. **Prepare the Turkey:** Season the turkey fillets with salt and pepper on both sides.
2. **Sealing:** Vacuum-seal the turkey fillets in bags, adding minced garlic, olive oil, thyme, and rosemary to each bag. Seal the bags using a vacuum sealer.
3. **Sous Vide Cooking:** Preheat the Sous Vide water bath to 149°F (65°C). Place the bags with the turkey into the water and cook for 2 hours.
4. **Final Preparation:** Remove the bags from the water and carefully open them. Heat a skillet over medium heat with olive oil and butter. Sear the turkey fillets until golden brown, about 1-2 minutes on each side. Finish by drizzling with lemon juice.
5. **Serving:** Serve the turkey with a side of fresh vegetables or mashed potatoes, garnished with fresh herbs.

Cooking Time: 2 hours 20 minutes (including preparation and searing time)
Servings: 2

Serving Tips:

- Serve the turkey with a side of rice, quinoa, or mashed potatoes for added nutrition.
- For enhanced flavor, add a splash of white wine to the skillet during searing.

Nutritional Information per Serving: Calories: 350, Protein: 30 g, Fat: 20 g, Carbohydrates: 2 g

Side Dishes

Vegetable Stew

Ingredients:

- 1 small zucchini, diced
- 1 red bell pepper, sliced
- 1 small carrot, diced
- 1 cup broccoli florets (240 ml)
- 1 onion, sliced into half-moons
- 2 garlic cloves, minced

- 2 tablespoons olive oil (30 ml)
- 1 teaspoon dried thyme (5 ml)
- 1 teaspoon dried oregano (5 ml)
- Salt and pepper to taste

Instructions:

1. Prepare the Ingredients: In a bowl, combine the diced zucchini, sliced bell pepper, diced carrot, broccoli florets, sliced onion, minced garlic, olive oil, thyme, oregano, salt, and pepper.
2. Sealing: Transfer the mixture to a vacuum-seal bag and seal it using a vacuum sealer.
3. Sous Vide Cooking: Preheat the Sous Vide water bath to 185°F (85°C). Place the bag with the vegetable mixture into the water and cook for 1 hour.
4. Final Preparation: Remove the bag from the water and carefully open it. Transfer the vegetable stew to a serving plate and serve hot.

Cooking Time: 1 hour 20 minutes (including preparation and cooling time)
Servings: 2-3

Serving Tips:

- Serve the vegetable stew as a standalone dish or as a side dish to complement a main course.
- For added flavor, drizzle some fresh lemon juice over the stew before serving.

Nutritional Information per Serving: Calories: 150, Protein: 3 g, Fat: 10 g, Carbohydrates: 12 g

Ingredients:

- 500 g (about 1 lb) potatoes, cubed
- 2 tablespoons olive oil
- 2 cloves garlic, minced
- 1 teaspoon dried rosemary

- 1 teaspoon dried thyme
- Salt and pepper to taste
- Fresh parsley for garnish

Instructions:

1. **Prepare the Potatoes:** In a bowl, mix the cubed potatoes with olive oil, minced garlic, rosemary, thyme, salt, and pepper.
2. **Seal:** Vacuum seal the potatoes in bags using a vacuum sealer.
3. **Sous Vide Cooking:** Preheat the Sous Vide water bath to 85°C (185°F). Place the sealed potato bags into the water and cook for 1.5 hours.
4. **Final Preparation:** Remove the bags from the water and carefully open them. Transfer the potatoes to a baking sheet and bake in a preheated oven at 220°C (425°F) until golden brown, about 10-15 minutes.
5. **Serve:** Serve the baked potatoes hot, garnished with fresh parsley.

Cooking Time: 2 hours (including preparation and baking time)
Servings: 3-4

Serving Tips: • Serve the baked potatoes as a side dish to meat or fish. • For added flavor, sprinkle some Parmesan cheese before serving.

Nutritional Information per Serving: Calories: 200, Protein: 3 g, Fat: 10 g, Carbohydrates: 25 g

Ingredients:

- 500 g (about 1 lb) asparagus, trimmed
- 2 tablespoons olive oil
- Juice of 1 lemon
- Zest of 1 lemon

- 2 cloves garlic, minced
- Salt and pepper to taste
- Fresh dill for garnish

Instructions:

1. **Prepare the Asparagus:** In a bowl, mix the asparagus, olive oil, lemon juice and zest, minced garlic, salt, and pepper.
2. **Seal:** Vacuum seal the asparagus in bags using a vacuum sealer.
3. **Sous Vide Cooking:** Preheat the Sous Vide water bath to 85°C (185°F). Place the sealed asparagus bags into the water and cook for 30 minutes.
4. **Final Preparation:** Remove the bags from the water and carefully open them. Transfer the asparagus to a plate and serve hot.
5. **Serve:** Garnish the asparagus with fresh dill.

Cooking Time: 45 minutes (including preparation and cooling time)
Servings: 2-3

Serving Tips: • Serve the asparagus as a side dish to meat or fish. • For added flavor, sprinkle some grated Parmesan cheese before serving.

Nutritional Information per Serving: Calories: 100, Protein: 2 g, Fat: 7 g, Carbohydrates: 8 g

Brussels Sprouts

Ingredients:

- 1 lb Brussels sprouts, trimmed and halved
- 2 tablespoons olive oil
- 3 garlic cloves, minced
- 1 tablespoon balsamic vinegar
- Salt and pepper to taste
- Pinch of red pepper flakes (optional)
- Fresh parsley for garnish

Instructions:

1. **Preparing the Brussels Sprouts:** In a bowl, mix the Brussels sprouts, olive oil, minced garlic, balsamic vinegar, salt, pepper, and red pepper flakes (if using).
2. **Sealing:** Vacuum seal the Brussels sprouts in bags using a vacuum sealer.
3. **Sous Vide Cooking:** Preheat the Sous Vide machine to 185°F (85°C). Place the bags with Brussels sprouts in the water and cook for 1 hour.
4. **Final Preparation:** Remove the bags from the water and carefully open them. Transfer the Brussels sprouts to a baking sheet and roast in a preheated oven at 425°F (220°C) until golden brown, about 10-15 minutes.
5. **Serving:** Serve the Brussels sprouts hot, garnished with fresh parsley.

Cooking Time: 1 hour 30 minutes (including preparation and roasting time)
Servings: 3-4

Serving Tips:

- Serve the Brussels sprouts as a side dish with meat or fish dishes.
- For added flavor, sprinkle some grated Parmesan before serving.

Nutritional Information per Serving: Calories: 150, Protein: 4 g, Fat: 10 g, Carbohydrates: 12 g

Garlic and Herb Mushrooms

Ingredients:

- 1 lb mushrooms, halved
- 3 garlic cloves, minced
- 2 tablespoons olive oil
- 1 tablespoon butter
- 1 teaspoon dried thyme

- 1 teaspoon dried rosemary
- Salt and pepper to taste
- Fresh parsley for garnish

Instructions:

1. **Preparing the Mushrooms:** In a bowl, mix the halved mushrooms, minced garlic, olive oil, butter, thyme, rosemary, salt, and pepper.
2. **Sealing:** Vacuum seal the mushrooms in bags using a vacuum sealer.
3. **Sous Vide Cooking:** Preheat the Sous Vide machine to 185°F (85°C). Place the bags with the mushrooms in the water and cook for 1 hour.
4. **Final Preparation:** Remove the bags from the water and carefully open them. Transfer the mushrooms to a skillet and sauté over medium heat until golden brown, about 5 minutes.
5. **Serving:** Serve the mushrooms hot, garnished with fresh parsley.

Cooking Time: 1 hour 15 minutes (including preparation and sautéing time)
Servings: 3-4

Serving Tips:

- Serve the mushrooms as a side dish with meat or fish dishes.
- For added flavor, drizzle a bit of balsamic vinegar before serving.

Nutritional Information per Serving: Calories: 150, Protein: 4 g, Fat: 10 g, Carbohydrates: 8 g

Honey Thyme Carrots

Ingredients:

- 1 lb carrots, sliced into rounds or sticks
- 2 tablespoons honey
- 2 tablespoons olive oil
- 1 teaspoon dried thyme
- Salt and pepper to taste
- Fresh parsley for garnish

Instructions:

1. **Preparing the Carrots:** In a bowl, mix the sliced carrots, honey, olive oil, thyme, salt, and pepper.
2. **Sealing:** Vacuum seal the carrots in bags using a vacuum sealer.
3. **Sous Vide Cooking:** Preheat the Sous Vide machine to 185°F (85°C). Place the bags with the carrots in the water and cook for 1 hour.
4. **Final Preparation:** Remove the bags from the water and carefully open them. Transfer the carrots to a baking sheet and roast in a preheated oven at 425°F (220°C) until golden brown, about 10-15 minutes.
5. **Serving:** Serve the carrots hot, garnished with fresh parsley.

Cooking Time: 1 hour 30 minutes (including preparation and roasting time)
Servings: 3-4

Serving Tips:
- Serve the carrots as a side dish with meat or fish dishes.
- For added flavor, drizzle a bit of balsamic vinegar before serving.

Nutritional Information per Serving: Calories: 120, Protein: 1 g, Fat: 7 g, Carbohydrates: 15 g

Ingredients:

- 1 lb sweet potatoes, cubed
- 2 tablespoons olive oil
- 1 tablespoon maple syrup
- 1 teaspoon ground cinnamon
- 1/2 teaspoon ground nutmeg
- Salt and pepper to taste
- Fresh parsley for garnish

Instructions:

1. **Preparing the Sweet Potatoes:** In a bowl, mix the cubed sweet potatoes, olive oil, maple syrup, cinnamon, nutmeg, salt, and pepper.
2. **Sealing:** Vacuum seal the sweet potatoes in bags using a vacuum sealer.
3. **Sous Vide Cooking:** Preheat the Sous Vide machine to 185°F (85°C). Place the bags with the sweet potatoes in the water and cook for 1 hour.
4. **Final Preparation:** Remove the bags from the water and carefully open them. Transfer the sweet potatoes to a baking sheet and roast in a preheated oven at 425°F (220°C) until golden brown, about 10-15 minutes.
5. **Serving:** Serve the sweet potatoes hot, garnished with fresh parsley.

Cooking Time: 1 hour 30 minutes (including preparation and roasting time)
Servings: 3-4

Serving Tips:

- Serve the sweet potatoes as a side dish with meat or fish dishes.
- For added flavor, drizzle a bit of balsamic vinegar before serving.

Nutritional Information per Serving: Calories: 180, Protein: 2 g, Fat: 7 g, Carbohydrates: 28 g

Couscous with Vegetables

Ingredients:

- 1 cup couscous
- 1 1/4 cups vegetable broth
- 1 small carrot, diced
- 1 red bell pepper, diced
- 1 small zucchini, diced
- 1/2 cup green peas

- 2 tablespoons olive oil
- 2 cloves garlic, minced
- Salt and pepper to taste
- Fresh parsley for garnish

Instructions:

1. **Preparing Ingredients:** In a bowl, combine couscous, vegetable broth, diced carrot, red bell pepper, zucchini, green peas, olive oil, minced garlic, salt, and pepper.
2. **Sealing:** Vacuum seal the mixture in a bag using a vacuum sealer.
3. **Sous Vide Cooking:** Preheat the Sous Vide machine to 185°F (85°C). Place the bag with the couscous and vegetables in the water and cook for 30 minutes.
4. **Final Preparation:** Remove the bag from the water and carefully open it. Transfer the couscous with vegetables to a plate and serve hot, garnished with fresh parsley.

Cooking Time: 45 minutes (including preparation and cooling time)
Servings: 2-3

Serving Tips:

- Serve the couscous with vegetables as a main dish or as a side dish to meat or fish dishes.
- For added flavor, you can drizzle a bit of lemon juice before serving.

Nutritional Information per Serving: Calories: 220, Protein: 5 g, Fat: 8 g, Carbohydrates: 30 g

Baked Tomatoes with Basil

Ingredients:

- 500 g cherry tomatoes, halved
- 2 tablespoons olive oil
- 3 cloves garlic, minced
- 1 tablespoon balsamic vinegar
- Salt and pepper to taste
- Fresh basil for garnish

Instructions:

1. **Preparing the Tomatoes:** In a bowl, combine the cherry tomatoes, olive oil, minced garlic, balsamic vinegar, salt, and pepper.
2. **Sealing:** Vacuum seal the tomatoes in bags using a vacuum sealer.
3. **Sous Vide Cooking:** Preheat the Sous Vide machine to 185°F (85°C). Place the bags with the tomatoes in the water and cook for 45 minutes.
4. **Final Preparation:** Remove the bags from the water and carefully open them. Transfer the tomatoes to a baking sheet and bake in a preheated oven at 425°F (220°C) until soft and slightly caramelized, about 10-15 minutes.
5. **Serving:** Serve the baked tomatoes hot, garnished with fresh basil.

Cooking Time: 1 hour (including preparation and baking time)
Servings: 2-3

Serving Tips:

- Serve the baked tomatoes as a side dish to meat or fish dishes.
- For added flavor, you can sprinkle some grated Parmesan before serving.

Nutritional Information per Serving: Calories: 120, Protein: 2 g, Fat: 8 g, Carbohydrates: 10 g

Cauliflower with Turmeric

Ingredients:

- 1 head cauliflower, cut into florets
- 2 tablespoons olive oil
- 1 teaspoon ground turmeric
- 1/2 teaspoon ground cumin
- Salt and pepper to taste
- Fresh parsley for garnish

Instructions:

1. **Preparing the Cauliflower:** In a bowl, mix the cauliflower florets, olive oil, ground turmeric, ground cumin, salt, and pepper.
2. **Sealing:** Vacuum seal the cauliflower in bags using a vacuum sealer.
3. **Sous Vide Cooking:** Preheat the Sous Vide machine to 185°F (85°C). Place the bags with the cauliflower in the water and cook for 1 hour.
4. **Final Preparation:** Remove the bags from the water and carefully open them. Transfer the cauliflower to a baking sheet and bake in a preheated oven at 425°F (220°C) until golden brown, about 10-15 minutes.
5. **Serving:** Serve the cauliflower hot, garnished with fresh parsley.

Cooking Time: 1 hour 30 minutes (including preparation and baking time)
Servings: 3-4

Serving Tips:

- Serve the cauliflower as a side dish to meat or fish dishes.
- For added flavor, you can drizzle some lemon juice before serving.

Nutritional Information per Serving: Calories: 100, Protein: 3 g, Fat: 7 g, Carbohydrates: 7 g

Desserts

Fruit Compotes

Ingredients:

- 2 apples, peeled and sliced
- 2 pears, peeled and sliced
- 1 cup berries (raspberries, blueberries, strawberries)
- 1/2 cup water

- 1/4 cup honey or maple syrup
- 1 cinnamon stick
- 1 teaspoon vanilla extract
- Fresh mint for garnish

Instructions:

1. **Prepare the fruit:** In a bowl, mix the sliced apples, pears, and berries.
2. **Sealing:** Vacuum seal the fruits in bags, adding water, honey or maple syrup, the cinnamon stick, and vanilla extract. Seal the bags using a vacuum sealer.
3. **Sous Vide Cooking:** Preheat the Sous Vide machine to 185°F (85°C). Place the bags with the fruits in the water and cook for 1 hour.
4. **Final Preparation:** Remove the bags from the water and carefully open them. Transfer the fruits and liquid to a serving bowl.
5. **Serving:** Serve the fruit compotes warm or chilled, garnished with fresh mint.

Cooking Time: 1 hour 15 minutes (including preparation and cooling time)
Servings: 4-5

Serving Tips: • Serve the fruit compotes with yogurt or ice cream. • For a more intense flavor, add a bit of lemon juice before serving.

Nutritional Information per Serving: Calories: 120, Protein: 1 g, Fat: 0 g, Carbohydrates: 31 g

Ingredients:

- 2 cups Greek yogurt
- 1/4 cup honey or maple syrup
- 1 teaspoon vanilla extract
- 1 cup fresh berries (raspberries, blueberries, strawberries)
- 1/4 cup granola for garnish
- Fresh mint for garnish

Instructions:

1. **Prepare the yogurt:** In a bowl, mix Greek yogurt, honey or maple syrup, and vanilla extract.
2. **Sealing:** Vacuum seal the yogurt in bags and seal them using a vacuum sealer.
3. **Sous Vide Cooking:** Preheat the Sous Vide machine to 113°F (45°C). Place the bags with the yogurt in the water and cook for 6 hours.
4. **Final Preparation:** Remove the bags from the water and carefully open them. Transfer the yogurt to serving glasses or bowls.
5. **Serving:** Serve the yogurt desserts, garnished with fresh berries, granola, and fresh mint.

Cooking Time: 6 hours 15 minutes (including preparation and cooling time)
Servings: 4-5

Serving Tips:
• Serve the yogurt desserts with honey or maple syrup for additional sweetness.
• For a more intense flavor, add a bit of lemon juice before serving.

Nutritional Information per Serving: Calories: 150, Protein: 8 g, Fat: 5 g, Carbohydrates: 18 g

Crème Brûlée

Ingredients:

- 2 cups heavy cream
- 1 vanilla bean (or 1 teaspoon vanilla extract)
- 5 egg yolks
- 1/2 cup sugar
- Additional sugar for caramelization
- Fresh berries and mint for garnish

Instructions:

1. Prepare Vanilla Cream: In a small saucepan, heat the cream and the split vanilla bean (or vanilla extract) over medium heat until it just begins to boil. Remove from heat and let it steep for 10 minutes. Remove the vanilla bean.
2. Mix Ingredients: In a bowl, whisk the egg yolks and sugar until smooth. Gradually pour the warm cream into the egg mixture, stirring constantly.
3. Sealing: Pour the mixture into vacuum bags or jars and seal them using a vacuum sealer.
4. Sous Vide Cooking: Preheat the Sous Vide machine to 180°F (82°C). Place the bags or jars in the water and cook for 1 hour.
5. Cooling: Remove the crème brûlée from the water and let it cool to room temperature, then refrigerate for 4 hours or overnight.
6. Caramelization: Before serving, sprinkle a thin layer of sugar on top of the crème brûlée and caramelize using a kitchen torch until a golden crust forms.
7. Serving: Serve the crème brûlée, garnished with fresh berries and mint.

Cooking Time: 5 hours (including cooling time)

Servings: 4

Serving Tips:

• Serve crème brûlée with additional berries or fruits.

• For a richer flavor, use brown sugar for caramelization.

Nutritional Information per Serving: Calories: 300, Protein: 4 g, Fat: 25 g, Carbohydrates: 18 g

Coconut Pudding

Ingredients:

- 2 cups coconut milk
- 1/4 cup honey or maple syrup
- 1 teaspoon vanilla extract
- 3 tablespoons cornstarch
- 1/4 cup shredded coconut
- Fresh berries for garnish
- Fresh mint for garnish

Instructions:

1. **Prepare Mixture:** In a bowl, mix coconut milk, honey or maple syrup, vanilla extract, and cornstarch until smooth.
2. **Sealing:** Pour the mixture into vacuum bags or jars and seal them using a vacuum sealer.
3. **Sous Vide Cooking:** Preheat the Sous Vide machine to 185°F (85°C). Place the bags or jars in the water and cook for 1 hour.
4. **Cooling:** Remove the bags or jars from the water and let them cool to room temperature, then refrigerate for 2 hours or overnight.
5. **Serving:** Serve the coconut pudding, garnished with fresh berries, shredded coconut, and mint.

Cooking Time: 3 hours (including cooling time)

Servings: 4

Serving Tips: • Serve coconut pudding with honey or maple syrup for extra sweetness. • For a richer flavor, add a bit of lemon juice before serving.

Nutritional Information per Serving: Calories: 200, Protein: 2 g, Fat: 12 g, Carbohydrates: 22 g

Banana Mousse

Ingredients:

- 3 ripe bananas, sliced
- 1 cup heavy cream
- 1/4 cup honey or maple syrup
- 1 teaspoon vanilla extract
- 1 tablespoon lemon juice
- Fresh berries for garnish
- Fresh mint for garnish

Instructions:

1. **Prepare Mixture:** In a blender, combine sliced bananas, heavy cream, honey or maple syrup, vanilla extract, and lemon juice until smooth.
2. **Sealing:** Pour the mixture into vacuum bags or jars and seal them using a vacuum sealer.
3. **Sous Vide Cooking:** Preheat the Sous Vide machine to 185°F (85°C). Place the bags or jars in the water and cook for 1 hour.
4. **Cooling:** Remove the bags or jars from the water and let them cool to room temperature, then refrigerate for 2 hours or overnight.
5. **Serving:** Serve the banana mousse, garnished with fresh berries and mint.

Cooking Time: 3 hours (including cooling time)

Servings: 4

Serving Tips: • Serve banana mousse with additional berries or fruits. • For a richer flavor, add some grated chocolate before serving.

Nutritional Information per Serving: Calories: 220, Protein: 2 g, Fat: 10 g, Carbohydrates: 30 g

Drinks and Sauces

Vanilla Homemade Yogurt

Ingredients:

- 4 cups whole milk
- 1/2 cup Greek yogurt (as a starter)
- 1/4 cup honey or maple syrup
- 1 teaspoon vanilla extract

Instructions:

1. **Milk Preparation:** In a small saucepan, heat the milk to 185°F (85°C). Remove from heat and let cool to 110°F (43°C).
2. **Mixing Ingredients:** In a bowl, mix the cooled milk with Greek yogurt, honey or maple syrup, and vanilla extract until smooth.
3. **Sealing:** Vacuum seal the mixture in bags or pour into glass jars and seal them using a vacuum sealer.
4. **Sous Vide Cooking:** Preheat the Sous Vide machine to 110°F (43°C). Place the bags or jars with the yogurt mixture into the water and cook for 6-8 hours.
5. **Cooling:** Remove the bags or jars from the water and let cool to room temperature, then refrigerate for 4 hours or overnight.
6. **Serving:** Serve the homemade vanilla yogurt, garnished with fresh berries or fruits if desired.

Total Time: 12 hours (including cooling)

Servings: 4

Serving Tips: • Serve the yogurt with honey, nuts, or muesli for added nutrition. • For a richer flavor, add a bit of cinnamon or cardamom before serving.

Nutrition per Serving: Calories: 150, Protein: 8 g, Fat: 6 g, Carbohydrates: 18 g

Vanilla Extract

Ingredients:

- 3 vanilla beans
- 1 cup vodka (or another strong alcohol, such as rum or bourbon)

Instructions:

1. **Preparing the Vanilla Beans:** Split the vanilla beans lengthwise and carefully open them to expose the seeds.
2. **Sealing:** Place the split vanilla beans in a vacuum bag or glass jar. Add the vodka and seal the bag or jar using a vacuum sealer.
3. **Sous Vide Cooking:** Preheat the Sous Vide machine to 135°F (57°C). Place the bag or jar with the vanilla mixture into the water and cook for 2 hours.
4. **Cooling:** Remove the bag or jar from the water and let it cool to room temperature. Leave the extract to steep at room temperature for an additional 1 week for a more intense flavor.
5. **Usage:** The vanilla extract is ready to use. Store it in a tightly sealed jar in a cool, dark place.

Total Time: 2 hours + 1 week steeping

Yield: 1 cup vanilla extract

Usage Tips: • Use the vanilla extract in baking, desserts, and beverages. • For a stronger flavor, you can add more vanilla beans and increase the steeping time.

Nutrition per Serving: Calories: 0, Protein: 0 g, Fat: 0 g, Carbohydrates: 0 g

Passion Fruit Smoothie

Ingredients:

- 2 ripe passion fruits
- 1 ripe banana
- 1 cup coconut milk
- 1/2 cup Greek yogurt
- 1 tablespoon honey or maple syrup
- 1 teaspoon vanilla extract
- Ice to taste
- Fresh mint for garnish

Instructions:

1. **Preparing Ingredients:** Cut the passion fruits in half and scoop out the pulp.
2. **Blending Ingredients:** In a blender, combine the passion fruit pulp, sliced banana, coconut milk, Greek yogurt, honey or maple syrup, vanilla extract, and ice. Blend until smooth.
3. **Sealing:** Vacuum-seal the mixture in bags and seal them using a vacuum sealer.
4. **Sous Vide Cooking:** Preheat the Sous Vide machine to 131°F (55°C). Place the bags with the passion fruit smoothie into the water and cook for 30 minutes.
5. **Cooling:** Remove the bags from the water and let them cool to room temperature. Transfer the smoothie to serving glasses.
6. **Serving:** Serve the passion fruit smoothie garnished with fresh mint.

Total Time: 1 hour (including cooling)

Servings: 2

Serving Tips: • Serve the passion fruit smoothie with additional fruits or berries. • For a more intense flavor, add a little lemon juice before serving.

Nutrition per Serving: Calories: 180, Protein: 4 g, Fat: 5 g, Carbohydrates: 30 g

Lemon Curd

Ingredients:

- 3 large eggs
- 3/4 cup sugar
- 1/2 cup fresh lemon juice (about 3-4 lemons)
- 1 tablespoon lemon zest
- 1/2 cup butter, cut into cubes

Instructions:

1. **Mixing Ingredients:** In a bowl, whisk together the eggs and sugar until smooth. Add the lemon juice, lemon zest, and butter, and whisk until well combined.
2. **Sealing:** Pour the mixture into a vacuum-seal bag and seal it using a vacuum sealer.
3. **Sous Vide Cooking:** Preheat the Sous Vide machine to 180°F (82°C). Place the bag with the lemon mixture into the water and cook for 1 hour, occasionally stirring the mixture through the bag.
4. **Cooling:** Remove the bag from the water and carefully open it. Transfer the lemon curd to a clean bowl and let it cool to room temperature, then refrigerate for 2 hours or overnight.
5. **Serving:** Serve the lemon curd as a dessert or use it in baking, garnished with fresh berries and mint.

Total Time: 3 hours (including cooling)

Yield: 2 cups lemon curd

Serving Tips: • Serve the lemon curd with biscuits, toast, or as a filling for pies. • For a more intense flavor, you can add a little lemon juice before serving.

Nutrition per Serving: Calories: 150, Protein: 3 g, Fat: 10 g, Carbohydrates: 15 g

Mango Tea Smoothie

Ingredients:

- 1 ripe mango, cubed
- 1 cup green tea, brewed and chilled
- 1/2 cup coconut milk
- 1 tablespoon honey or maple syrup
- 1 teaspoon vanilla extract
- Ice to taste
- Fresh mint for garnish

Instructions:

1. **Preparing Ingredients:** In a blender, combine the cubed mango, brewed and chilled green tea, coconut milk, honey or maple syrup, vanilla extract, and ice until smooth.
2. **Sealing:** Pour the mixture into vacuum-seal bags and seal them using a vacuum sealer.
3. **Sous Vide Cooking:** Preheat the Sous Vide machine to 131°F (55°C). Place the bags with the tea smoothie into the water and cook for 30 minutes.
4. **Cooling:** Remove the bags from the water and let them cool to room temperature. Transfer the smoothie to serving glasses.
5. **Serving:** Serve the mango tea smoothie garnished with fresh mint.

Total Time: 1 hour (including cooling)

Servings: 2

Serving Tips: • Serve the mango tea smoothie with additional fruits or berries. • For a more intense flavor, add a little lemon juice before serving.

Nutrition per Serving: Calories: 150, Protein: 2 g, Fat: 3 g, Carbohydrates: 30 g

Practical Tips and Recommendations

Safety and Hygiene Tips

Hygienic Principles: In the culinary world, where every detail matters, hygiene and safety are the foundation of your success. Always wash your hands before starting to cook and after handling raw foods. Use separate cutting boards and knives for raw and cooked foods to prevent cross-contamination. Keep your kitchen a place of cleanliness and order, where every dish is created with care and attention.

Food Storage Temperature: Store raw products in the refrigerator at 39°F (4°C) or below. Freeze products at 0°F (-18°C) or below. Never leave food at room temperature for more than two hours. These simple rules will help maintain the freshness and safety of your ingredients.

Proper Cooking: Ensure that the water in the sous-vide machine has reached the desired temperature before adding the food. Use a thermometer to check the internal temperature of the food, especially meat and fish, to ensure they are fully cooked. Your confidence in achieving the perfect result will grow with each dish you prepare.

Vacuum Sealing: Check the vacuum bags for leaks before use. Use high-quality vacuum bags designed for sous-vide cooking. Your food deserves the best protection to preserve its amazing flavors and textures.

Storage Duration of Cooked Dishes: Sous-vide cooked dishes can be stored in the refrigerator for no more than 3-4 days. Freeze cooked dishes for long-term storage, ensuring they are well-sealed. This will allow you to enjoy delicious and fresh meals anytime.

Cooling and Reheating: Cool hot dishes in the refrigerator as quickly as possible to prevent bacterial growth. Reheat cooked dishes to 165°F (74°C) before serving. Every dish served should not only be tasty but also safe for your loved ones.

Equipment Safety: Regularly check your sous-vide machine and other equipment for damage and malfunctions. Monitor the water level in the sous-vide machine during cooking to avoid overheating and equipment damage. The reliability of your equipment is the key to successful cooking.

By following these safety and hygiene tips, you will be able to create not only delicious but also safe dishes that will delight you and your loved ones. Let every meal be a source of health and pleasure.

Menu Planning: Every family meal starts with a well-thought-out menu. Create a weekly menu that includes a variety of dishes to satisfy the tastes of all family members. Let each day be filled with new culinary discoveries, and your loved ones will always look forward to the next meal.

Preparing Ingredients in Advance: Let your kitchen become a place where time works for you. Chop and prepare all ingredients in advance to speed up the cooking process. Store prepared ingredients in airtight containers in the refrigerator or freezer, so they are always at hand when you start cooking.

Family Involvement: Cooking can be a wonderful time for bonding and creativity. Involve children and other family members in the cooking process. Let everyone find their role in the kitchen, whether it's chopping vegetables, mixing ingredients, or garnishing the finished dish. Cooking together brings everyone closer and fills the home with warmth.

Recipe Adaptation: Every family is unique, and your recipes should reflect that. Adapt recipes according to the preferences and needs of each family member. Use different spices and seasonings to satisfy everyone's tastes. Let your dishes be as diverse and vibrant as your family.

Cooking Large Portions: Cook large portions of dishes so you can store them in the refrigerator or freezer for quick reheating on weekdays. Divide large portions into individual servings before freezing to simplify reheating and serving. This not only saves you time but also provides ready meals for several days ahead.

Interactive Meals: Create interactive meals such as build-your-own salads, tacos, or pizzas where each family member can choose their favorite ingredients. Use sous-vide to prepare the main ingredients in advance to simplify the assembly process. This turns every meal into a fun event that everyone will enjoy.

Maintaining Healthy Habits: Your health is your wealth. Include more vegetables, fruits, whole grains, and protein-rich foods in your diet. Limit your intake of sugar, salt, and saturated fats. Let every meal be a step towards health and longevity.

Experimenting with New Recipes: Don't be afraid to try something new. Regularly experiment with new recipes and cooking techniques to diversify the family menu. Involve all family members in choosing new recipes and planning meals. Let your kitchen become a place for culinary discoveries and delights.

By following these tips, you can create delicious and diverse dishes that cater to the tastes of every family member and make every meal special. Let your kitchen become the heart of your home, where love, flavor, and health reign.

Product	Cooking Time	Cooking Temperature
BEEF		
Raw Steak 20-30 mm	15-30 min	122°F (50°C)
Raw Steak 30-40 mm	25-30 min	122°F (50°C)
Rare Steak 20-30 mm	40-120 min	131°F (55°C)
Rare Steak 30-40 mm	65-120 min	131°F (55°C)
Medium Rare Steak 20-30 mm	45-180 min	136°F (58°C)
Medium Rare Steak 30-40 mm	80-180 min	136°F (58°C)
Ribs	60-240 min	136°F (58°C)
Beef tongue	18-24 hours	158°F (70°C)
PORK		
Pork loin	150-600 min	176°F (80°C)
Fillet 30-40 mm	65-120 min	140°F (60°C)
Fillet 40-50 mm	100-120 min	140°F (60°C)
Pork neck	600 min	167°F (75°C)
Cutting 20-30 mm	35-170 min	140°F (60°C)
Fillet 30-40 mm	60-170 min	140°F (60°C)
Ham	20 hours	149°F (65°C)
Shoulder	600 min	176°F (80°C)
Shank	300-420 min	158°F (70°C)
Kebab	120 min	158°F (70°C)
Belly	300 min	158°F (70°C)
LAMB		
Leg (Shank)	24 hours	153°F (67°C)
Fillet	180 min	136°F (58°C)
POULTRY		
Duck (Fillet)	90-150 min	136°F (58°C)
Duck (Legs)	130-240 min	176°F (80°C)
Goose Liver	30-45 min	131°F (55°C)
Goose (Legs)	70-130 min	136°F (58°C)
Chicken (Fillet)	40-70 min	149°F (65°C)
Chicken (Legs)	180 min	149°F (65°C)
Turkey (Fillet)	70-120 min	149°F (65°C)
RABBIT		
Rabbit (Fillet)	240 min	144°F (62°C)
Rabbit (Legs)	600 min	147°F (64°C)
EGGS		
Soft Boiled	60 min	149°F (65°C)
Hard Boiled	80 min	154°F (68°C)
Poached	60 min	144°F (62°C)
FISH & SEAFOOD		
Salmon	15-25 min	122°F (50°C)
Sole	15-30 min	126°F (52°C)
Halibut	15-30 min	126°F (52°C)
Tuna	20-50 min	136°F (58°C)

Perch	15-60 min	126°F (52°C)
Catfish	60 min	122°F (50°C)
Mackerel	10-15 min	126°F (52°C)
Octopus	240 min	185°F (85°C)
Shrimp	25 min	122°F (50°C)
Lobster	30-60 min	136°F (58°C)

VEGETABLES

Cabbage	60 min	185°F (85°C)
Carrot	50 min	185°F (85°C)
Corn	60 min	185°F (85°C)
Green Beans	120 min	185°F (85°C)
Mushrooms	15 min	185°F (85°C)
Potato	50 min	185°F (85°C)
Turnip	60 min	185°F (85°C)
Asparagus	35-55 min	185°F (85°C)
Lettuce	60 min	185°F (85°C)
Celery	90 min	185°F (85°C)
Pumpkin	10-95 min	185°F (85°C)

FRUITS

Cherry	25 min	158°F (70°C)
Pear	25 min	185°F (85°C)
Plum	25 min	158°F (70°C)
Apple	25-35 min	185°F (85°C)
Berries	45 min	158°F (70°C)

Cook with joy!!!

Dear Readers,

Thank you for choosing this book. I hope it becomes your reliable companion on the path to a healthy and happy future. May every day be filled with aroma, taste, and health.

If you found value in this book, please consider leaving a review on Amazon. Your support through reviews helps us reach more people who might benefit from this guide.

https://www.amazon.com/review/create-review/?ie=UTF8&channel=glance-detail&asin=B0D93LMWSY

To do this, scan this QR code and fill out all the fields of the form, then click submit.

All the author's books can be found here:

https://www.amazon.com/stores/Yurii-Sreda/author/B0CSFS13NB?ref=ap_rdr&isDramIntegrated=true&shoppingPortalEnabled=true

With best wishes,
Yurii Sreda

Our contacts:
Telegram, WhatsApp, Viber
Yuriii Sreda +380503016500 email: syg25466@gmail.com
Inna Sreda +380504040668 email: innasreda@gmail.com

Yurii & Inna Sreda

Transformative Nutrition:
Comprehensive Guides to Healthy Eating,
Weight Loss, and Sustainable Wellness

 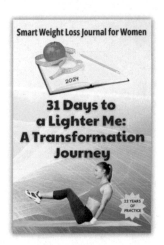 

Find more books on the author's page here

Made in United States
Troutdale, OR
11/17/2024

24964934R00042